# Lipstick, Heels & Hustle

## A Woman's Guide to Entrepreneurship

### By

### Dr. Carey D. Yazeed

Shero Books
A Subsidiary of Shero Productions
Baton Rouge, Louisiana

Shero Books, P.O. Box 84066, Baton Rouge, LA 70884
Lipstick, Heels & Hustle: A Woman's Guide
to Entrepreneurship
All Rights Reserved. Copyright 2017 by Dr. Carey Yazeed
Edited by: Editorhelen/fiverr
For information on booking the author for book signings
and speaking events:
drcareyyazeed@gmail.com
ISBN: 978-0-9850316-3-3
Printed in the United States of America

*This book is dedicated to my line sisters,*
*46 Devastating Divas*
*Delta Sigma Theta Sorority, Inc.*
*Spring 2002*
*Baton Rouge Delta Alumnae Chapter*
*(Don't let all of the pink fool ya!)*

Laurie
Always follow
your dreams!
Dr. Camy Yoyard

*"Many receive advice, only the wise profit from it."*

**Harper Lee**

# *Introduction*

I started writing Lipstick, Heels & Hustle as a way to document my entrepreneurial journey, but somewhere along the way, it stopped being about me and more about you, the reader. As I worked with women like yourself, helping them to understand their journey into entrepreneurship, I slowly began to realize that all of us face the same obstacles, fears, and concerns when leaving our 9 to 5's and transition into becoming our own boss. I also began to notice that most of the resources and materials that address female entrepreneurs are really male oriented with the color pink slapped on top of them. I didn't like what I was seeing, so I decided to use this as an opportunity to change the narrative for women.

When I started out on my entrepreneurial journey, there wasn't a how-to guide. For over 30 years as the owner and operator of several successful businesses, I had to learn through trial and error. Most of my businesses made it past the five-year mark, which indicates success and profits, but I'll be honest, I've had a few that did not. Today all of the lessons I've learned over the years have allowed me to run a successful publishing company, which houses all of the books that I've written and to work from my home office as a virtual business strategist. So yes, when it comes to business, I can honestly say I know a thing or two about starting and maintaining one.

Everyday isn't a bed of roses, but the feeling of success, ownership and being in control of my own destiny is why I never looked back after leaving my 9 to 5 job to become a full-time entrepreneur, and I want to share that with you. This book is a simple how-to guide of what it takes to be a successful entrepreneur, how to use the resources that you have to help get you to the next level, whatever your next level may be, and the importance of constant, yet positive energy. This book is about what it takes to become a successful female entrepreneur and what it will take to keep you going. So grab your lipstick and heels and let's get down to business!

"*A woman is like a tea bag; you can't tell how strong she is until you put her in hot water.*"

**Eleanor Roosevelt**

## *Chapter One*

So why are so many women turning to entrepreneurship? I can answer that with one word–freedom. I grew up in a household with parents who ran their own catering company on the side while working 40 plus hours a week at a 9 to 5 so we could survive. My parents instilled in me the importance of having your own, and so I did. At the age of eleven, I started selling candy out of my backpack at school because we didn't have vending machines and the lunch usually sucked. I also sold pencils, loose-leaf paper and I loaned my peer's lunch money and charged interest if they were late repaying me. The financial freedom that I experienced at that young age allowed me to take care of myself, and my younger brother, and purchase items that my parents couldn't afford or that they deemed were not necessities. Financially, I could walk into a store and buy a Gucci purse, no questions asked. I wore the latest fashion and took trips with my friends if I wanted too because I was paying the cost to be my own boss. I made sure my brother and I never went without food and were able to experience life through the same lens as our middle-class friends.

I learned early on that when you fill a void, solve a problem or eliminate the pain of others, you can make a profit. I also learned that when you have your own money you make it very hard for people to tell you no and you realize that you have the power to change your narrative and that nostalgic feeling of freedom is something that you want to keep experiencing over and over again because once you have a taste of freedom; the freedom to make decisions regarding your worth, the freedom to follow your gut and be right, and the freedom to use your time as it best serves you, you become addicted. Your desire grows stronger to hold on to that freedom. So you do whatever it takes, you use whatever you have, to continue to edit your story until it ends the way that you want it too.

So I guess you are wondering what happened; how did I end up working in the field of social work for 23 years barely making a salary of $48,000 a year. It's simple; I bought into the American dream that was being sold at the time; go to school and get a good job. Somewhere along the way, I began to believe that a good job would be better than owning a business and I fell into the 9 to 5 trap. But throughout my career, I never remained on a job past two years. I was always unhappy, longing for more, hoping for the best. But the best never came, at least not on a job. I was making a lot of money for agencies, and revitalizing educational programs at universities, but in private, I was struggling financially to survive. Emotionally, I kept finding myself dealing with coworkers who saw me as a threat; a know it all, a show-off. Meanwhile, I just wanted the opportunity to showcase my skills and talents and be compensated so I could provide for myself, and my two sons.

When things got bad at one job, I would just pack up and find another one. I was always in search of that feeling that entrepreneurship gave me at an early age. My saving grace became my private mental health practice, which I did on the side, but after 20 years of hearing heartbreaking stories I eventually burned out. I also had experienced a nervous breakdown, which was brought on by several harassment incidents at my last place of employment. Honestly, I had tried to leave that job on numerous occasions. I applied for other teaching and administrative positions in higher education, but unlike in my younger years, the interviews didn't come and I found myself feeling stuck in a dead end job with no future. Ageism, sexism, and racism had finally caught up with me. A black female with a Ph.D., seeking employment in a white male dominated world, I soon began to realize that employers could hire younger talent at a cheaper price. I didn't stand a chance.

I truly believe that God gives us signs, but we sometimes ignore them when they don't fit into our plans. I saw these as signs that it was time for me to leave the field of social work, private practice, higher education and the 9 to 5 rat race altogether. So I took a leave of absence to try and get myself together and figure it all out. But God has a way of making sure you do as He wants you to do and so He allowed one more incident to take place in my professional life that would seal the deal of me walking away and never looking back.

The icing on the cake was when a former client from two years prior decided she wasn't happy with the counseling services I had provided to her, so she and her new therapist filed a complaint against me with the social work licensing board. I was devastated. All I thought I knew was how to be a clinical social worker, but in the blink of an eye, it was taken away from me. Even though I had notified the licensing board that I was no longer practicing, had given up my license and basically walked away from the field of social work altogether, I was still publically crucified. And it was in those humiliating moments that I knew never again would I put myself in a position where I had to answer to anyone except God and myself. I received the confirmation that He was giving to me, that it was time to stop trying to find happiness in a job and begin to create my own happiness through entrepreneurship.

In the end, my story had a happy ending. Since embracing entrepreneurship on a full time bases, my salary has increased, and I now determine my own work hours, which are centered around my two sons and their schedules. Mentally I am more engaged and able to give 100 percent of myself to projects and clients that appreciate what I bring to the table, and I have developed healthy relationships with individuals from around the globe, which as a social worker, my license limited me to only work with clients in the State of Louisiana. I also realized that in addition to being a great social worker, I am also a dynamic business owner that knows how to make money and a phenomenal teacher who is able to present information to various levels of learners so that everyone present understands. Entrepreneurship has allowed me the freedom to create the life that I've always wanted to live and knew I could live. I am no longer wondering, in search of freedom and happiness, because I've found it inside of me, through my skills, talents, and capabilities. My story is probably very different from yours and all of the other women who have sought out entrepreneurship for various reasons, but if we all sat around a campfire and shared our experiences, each story would end the same, with us talking about freedom.

*"You have what it takes to be a victorious, independent, fearless woman."*

**Tyra Banks**

## Chapter Two

The first step to starting a business is not what you are probably thinking. It is not coming up with a unique name that no other company has. It is not registering your business with the Secretary of State. And it is not applying for an EIN with the IRS so you can open a bank account. Yes, all of those steps are necessary, but none of them are where you should start. No, the first step is discovering your purpose and then your why.

Successful businesses are built on purpose. We are here for a reason. God has given each of us a purpose, and no two people have the same purpose, therefore, we are all unique. But what I have found to be true is that many don't know what their purpose is and hence, they start businesses that fail, because that is not where they were supposed to be, that was not their true gift or calling, and that was not what they were supposed to be doing. They were doing what they want to do, instead of what they were called to do.

Have you ever wondered what your purpose is? Like, have you sat there and tried to figure out what it is that God has called you to do? I always tell people, "The answer has always been there, you just never knew where to look or what questions to ask yourself." So here are three questions that I want you to take a moment and think about, then answer:

1. **What comes naturally to you?** Where others may struggle, what can you do easily, effortlessly, and without giving it a second thought?

2. **What do people ask you to do all the time?** Have you ever noticed that people are always coming to seek your assistance for one particular thing? Your purpose is visible to others, that's why they come to you for help.

3. **When people brag about you, what is that one thing they praise you for?** People are always singing your praises because they consider your purpose an asset! Your gift adds value to their lives, and it is because of that, that they uplift your name!

Take a moment and look at your answers. Do you see a pattern? What stands out the most to you?

Now I know what you're doing. You are sitting there saying, "but that's just a hobby, that's not my purpose, that's not a gift!"

And you are also saying, "And no one is going to pay me for that." Ahhhh that's the real issue, you don't see this as an asset, but other's do. And guess what, people will pay, you've just never stopped and asked them too. A true entrepreneur realizes what their gifts and talents are and how they can benefit others. Because these things come naturally to them, they tend to move faster than others, with a sense of urgency that others cannot match. Their talent is an art in a sense, because just like a piece by Pablo Picasso, some will try to imitate it, but they can never duplicate it. Your gifts and talents are unique to you and only you. Once you begin to realize this, you too will begin to see just how great you are.

So you still don't believe you are special? Well while you are sitting there doubting yourself, your purpose and what God has called you to do, I want you to pick up your smartphone and text 10 people. Ask each of them to describe you, using 5 verbs. They cannot use complete sentences, only words. Once you've received all of their text messages, I want you to sit down and on the same page that you answered the purpose questions I gave you earlier, I want you to write down all of the words that they used to describe you. Again, do you see a pattern? What word(s) are the most used? Yes, it's shocking when we see how others see us and show us what has been there all along. This, my dear, is your purpose! You are just as rare as an original Picasso painting. Embrace it!

Now for some, it's not that they don't know what their purpose is, they are simply not happy with their purpose. They don't want that to be their purpose, or they know what their purpose is but don't understand what they are supposed to do with it and so they run, and I can totally relate. My purpose is to motivate, inspire and uplift others, but especially women. I know this and I've lived by this, or so I thought, since becoming a professional. But the part that I ran from for many years was a ministry. All that I am, all that I hope for and all I will ever be, is tied to ministering. I grew up Catholic so I didn't get this part of my purpose and so I ran from it because I didn't understand it. I also didn't realize that as I ran, I was ministering. As I ran, I was empowering others, and hence, I had been walking in my purpose the entire time I thought I was running.

My classmate from Louisiana State University, Rev. Errol Dominque, helped me to wrap my head around this concept. He has been so patient over the years as I've sat in his office and asked a thousand questions about empowerment, ministering and becoming ordained. I am so grateful that he has the patience of Job because I know others would have grown weary of me. But Rev. Dominque would just lean back, nod and let me chat away and then he would point out that I had answered my own questions, lol. But it was moments like those when people just allowed me to talk and they listened, that the answers came to me. Once I figured out that God didn't want me in a pulpit and that He had been using me as He wanted me to serve, I stopped running and started serving even more!

I know my story about purpose isn't like yours and guess what, all of our stories are different, and they are supposed to be because none of us are the same. When trying to figure out what your purpose is, don't look at what others are doing, because that's not where the answer is. Look inside of you. Analyze what you do. Think about the activities that you enjoy. That's your purpose. I like to help people. I get excited teaching others and then watching them apply what I've taught them. I get an adrenaline rush when I see or hear the light bulb go off in a client's mind. That's what I live for! It's moments like those that an energetic feeling takes over me, one that I cannot describe, and that is what keeps me going. That is when you know you are walking in your purpose.

The other key ingredient to being a successful entrepreneur is knowing your "why." Why do you want to start a business? Why do you desire to be an entrepreneur? You can know your purpose and find a 9 to 5 job that will help you to fulfill it, so *why* do you want to be an entrepreneur? I find that people lie when they get to this fork in the road of being a business owner. They will say stuff like, "I want to give back, I want to make the world a better place, I love helping others, etc..." instead of being honest with themselves and admitting that they want a better quality of life, they want to spend more time with their family, they want the freedom to move around without any constraints.

The reason I've found that people give the "feel good statements" about starting a business is because society makes you feel bad if you say anything else. The world will have you thinking that you are selfish, immoral and materialistic for wanting to own and run a successful business and the reason for this is simple. We have been programmed to go to school, get an education and then work 20 years and retire on a pension. This way of thinking came about during the industrial age, where large companies needed workers and that was okay because there were jobs, good paying jobs that we were rewarded with once we graduated from college. But we are now in a technology age where the use of manpower to complete the work of big companies is becoming less needed. We now live in a world that requires one good programmer to tell a bunch of computers what to do and how to do it. The computers are a cheaper labor, compared to humans. So the notion of going to school and working until retirement is not realistic for millennials and generation Z and they understand that. The other problem with that statement is that baby boomers are still working. They are not retiring like society had predicted, which means generation X isn't being promoted into supervisory positions and are remaining in entry and mid-level positions longer. This also means that because they are stagnant in the workforce, there is no place for millennials and generation Z to start, so instead of waiting around for someone to give them a job, they are creating their own. So their reasons for starting businesses are not to hold hands while singing *Kumbaya my Lord*. These generations are becoming entrepreneurs to survive, to take care of their families, to have the quality of life that they were promised while growing up. They want the American dream too, but their journey to getting there is through entrepreneurship and not working in corporate America until they reach their mid 50's.

If you are going to be a successful entrepreneur, it is imperative that you know and understand your purpose for starting a business and also be completely honest about your "why." Do the hard work in the beginning and look at your strengths and weaknesses. Think about why people always reach out to you and how that makes you unique. Take a look at where you are right now when it comes to employment, quality of life and your happiness; is this where you want to be or do you want better? Ask yourself what will it take to allow you to finally live the life that you've always envisioned and then go out and create it!

*"I never dreamed about success, I worked for it"*

**Estee Lauder**

## *Chapter Three*

Many people don't ever start a business not because they lack the resources or don't know their purpose; they don't start one because they allow the fear of failing to get in their way. I watch as people come up with the worst case scenarios on why they shouldn't start a business and all of the things that *could* go wrong. But what they don't realize is that none of those things will probably go wrong, and the stuff that does go wrong serve as learning lessons that allow you and your business to grow.

I have never had the luxury to allow fear to stop me. Whenever I started a business, it HAD to work because I had invested every dime that I had to my name into it. Fear has also never stopped me from failing. Now poor choices and bad relationships have caused me to stumble and even close the doors to a business, but I never viewed those circumstances as failures. They were lessons that I needed to learn. They were doors that need to be closed and then deadbolt because I never needed to walk through them again. They also were not failures because I got back up and tried again. I never let fear stop me and neither should you.

If you are dealing with fear of failure, I want you to start working with a therapist, not a coach, a therapist. And I say this because something deep down inside of you is fueling your fear and you need to deal with it. Otherwise you will always have excuses and continue to remain stuck right where you are. Work with a therapist to help you to overcome and/or walk through your fears and began to face life head on. Too many times we don't move forward because we allow our fears to have control. Fear should never control you. You control the fear.

The second biggest fear that I hear from women wanting to become entrepreneurs is money. "I don't have enough money. That costs too much money. I'll never make any money." So let's deal with each of those. First, you will never have enough money. That's just the way of the world. But that also should not stop you from starting a business and investing in yourself. People say, "It takes money to make money," and yes, it does, but it doesn't take a lot of money to make a lot of money. If Jesus could take two fish and five loaves of bread to feed a large crowd, money is not an issue for you. It's called using what you have and making it multiply. You can't afford to register your business with the Secretary of State, cool. Take the five dollars that you have and build a book cover designed for the 20-page workbook you are going to sit at your computer and write and sell it online through Gumroad for five dollars. Advertise your workbook for free on social media and sell twenty copies. The five dollars that you started out with has now become $100. "It's that easy," you ask? Yes, it's that simple. Now you can take that $100 to go and register your business with the Secretary of State and guess what, your workbook has become passive income that will continue to generate revenue as long as you remind people that it is available.

Next, let's deal with "that costs too much." This is the mindset of a broke person, not a hustler. And not broke financially, but broken mentally and spiritually. You don't believe that God will provide a way for you to increase your gift. If that course, seminar or workshop costs too much, have you considered buying the book? Did you think about utilizing your local library? Have you ever sought out free consulting and mentorship from SCORE, a resource partner of the Small Business Administration in your area? The answer is probably no. And the answer is no because you are already living outside of your means, you see free as being beneath you, but let's go back to your gift and purpose, you've been giving away your goodies for free so someone saw you as an affordable resource and used you to help get themselves to their next level. When you say something "cost too much," take a moment and think about the purchases you've made recently. Did you go to the thrift store to buy an outfit for that interview or did you swipe your credit card for a $300 dress that you will probably wear only once? You spend your money on what you want and not what you need. So no, it doesn't cost too much, you just don't want to spend your money on it. You have got to change your mindset in order to become a successful entrepreneur. Sometimes that means you have to go without the fancy shoes with the matching purse and wear what you have in your closet and take that new outfit money and invest in the growth of your gift and your business. This is called priorities.

Lastly, I want to deal with, "I'll never make any money." And you're right! If you continue to speak that into existence, you won't make any money. If you're not serious about your business and knowing that it will take some money for you to make a lot of money then no, you will never make any money. The tongue is powerful, and if you use it incorrectly, it can kill you, but if used correctly, it can take you places you would never have imagined going. The next time you find yourself about to say, "I won't make any money," I want you to whip out one of the positive affirmations that I've included at the end of this chapter and say it instead. I want you to use these money affirmations throughout the day to help shift your mindset. You become what you think. If your brain hears positive affirmations about money your perspective about money will start to change, you will begin to attract money to you, and you will understand how Jesus was able to take two fish and five loaves of bread and feed all of those people. He was able to perform that miracle because he believed that he could.

Starting a business can be done on a budget. I just gave you an example with the electronic workbook. I've never spent a lot of money starting a business. I figured out what were the bare essentials that were needed, made a budget and tackled what I could when I could. I looked for unique opportunities that would allow me to make a small investment, but have a big return on my investment (ROI). When I didn't have enough money to attend a Lisa Nichols conference, I watched all of her videos on YouTube and checked out her book from the library, but I didn't let not having enough money stop me. When I started my podcast, I joined several Facebook groups for pod-casters, read the many posts and asked a thousand questions. I also turned to YouTube and Google for additional information, and in the end, I started my podcast for under $50. I use to pay astronomical amounts for graphic designs. Then my friend who is a trademark attorney pointed me in the direction of Fiverr, an online site that allows you to work with freelancers from around the world. I've worked with several professionals that I've found on Fiverr, and I can honestly tell you that for what I've paid in the past to have one book cover designed, I can now get a cover done, the manuscript formatted and promotional banners designed. I will take five dollars and make it multiple over and over again. Why, because I refuse to fail. I refuse to settle, and I refuse to go without.

It all starts with your mindset, how you perceive your situation, your desire to start a business and your willingness to get out there and do the necessary work. Are you willing to make that shift? Are you ready to do the internal hard work? All of these qualities become the colors that are used to make your business a masterpiece.

## Money Affirmations

*I release all resistance to attracting money*

*I am worthy of a positive cash flow*

*I am receiving money now with ease and grace*

*I chose to enjoy accepting payments*

*I am excited to be making money*

*The universe is conspiring to make me wealthy*

*I see myself living a life of financial security*

*My positive attitude is attracting money*

*I live confidently knowing I am worthy of prosperity*

*I am a wealthy and powerful woman*

*Money always finds its way to me*

*Success, money, and happiness come easily to me*

*I now live, feel and expect an abundance of money*

*My income is constantly increasing*

*I deserve to be well paid for my skills and my knowledge*

*Money flows to me from multiple sources*

*"Ninety percent of leadership is the ability to communicate something people want."*

**Dianne Feinstein**

# *Chapter Four*

L et's get something straight. Everybody isn't going to want what you have. It's easy to get excited once you've accepted your calling and begin to walk in your purpose by serving others through a business that you have started. It is also easy to get caught up in providing services that you think your ideal client wants or that you would like to have if you were the client. Well, I hate to burst your bubble, but that is the quickest way to fail.

Everyone doesn't need what you're offering. Only a small percentage of the world needs your services. It is imperative that you go into your new business knowing and understanding this. No need to get offended, it is just the reality of being in business and providing products and or services. Think about it, you don't want everything that everyone else is selling or providing, do you? Men don't visit an OBGYN for a yearly check-up, do they? Well, the same concept applies to your business. This is called finding your ideal client and having a niche.

Now once you've processed that, it's time to focus on who does want your services. Every business has an ideal client. This is the person whose problem your business solves. The worst thing a new business owner can do is guess. Please don't assume who you think your ideal client is, what keeps them up at night and what services they need and want from you. Do your research. A good business owner knows their customer inside and out. They know where they are, how they move and what makes them tick. They understand their pains and make sure they can supply them relief and a solution. This is a common mistake that many new business owners make, not knowing who their customer is and trying to work based off of assumptions. This is also why so many new businesses fail because the business owner doesn't take the time to study their subject, they don't understand that there is an art to selling and working with people.

Knowing who your customer is and what their needs are, allows you to niche down and specialize. This is what sets you apart from all of the other entrepreneurs who are on the virtual street corner offering the same products and services that you are. Once I figured out what my purpose was and that God wanted me to minister to women through entrepreneurship, I had to niche down. No, I don't work with men, no I don't work with all women. I work with professional women who are transitioning from their 9 to 5 jobs into entrepreneurship. That makes me unique. It makes me original and sets me apart from the thousands of business coaches and strategists that flood your social media timeline daily, fighting for your attention. Having a niche or specialization allows you to stand out from the crowd and be noticed.

Once you've decided what your specialty will be, the next step is to locate these special customers. This requires you to find groups that align with your purpose and then listen, ask questions and take notes. I call this gathering data; others may say it's people watching, while some probably call it cyberstalking. Whatever you want to call it, do it and gather the necessary information that you need to start developing products and services. You can also collect data by posting questions on social media. This gives your ideal client a voice and allows them to be a part of what you're doing. They are also more likely to buy from you because you actually implemented their suggestions and it is something they told you they need.

With all of my businesses, I have collected data that I have used to help better serve my customers and to create products and services that they would actually buy. While I ran my bookstore, I had a chart behind the counter that had various categories regarding urban book purchases. I was writing an urban fiction novel, and I wanted to know why customers selected certain books to read over others. The data that I collected revealed a pattern; purchases made by females were based on the color pink, the title of a book, how the story began, how it ended and the blurbs on the back cover. Once I compiled all of this information, I used it to create my book cover, develop strategic marketing materials and rewrite the books beginning and ending. I also changed the title from Out of Love to *Sideline Ho*. Why, because these were the factors that the readers of urban books used when deciding if they would make a purchase and I wanted them to purchase my book. If I would have assumed, I would have been way off and not made a dime. Instead, *Sideline Ho* went on to become an urban bestselling novel.

When I decided that I would begin to utilize my business knowledge and offer coaching and consulting services as a business strategist, I created a free survey using Survey Monkey. I figured out the information I needed that would help me to determine who my ideal client was, and I posted a link to the survey on LinkedIn because I knew this was the social media platform where my ideal client came to gain business knowledge. 100 people completed the survey, and afterwards, I looked at all of their answers and gained some valuable insight. Now I can describe my ideal client down to her toes, and every product that I create is for her.

When developing new programs for my ideal client, I always start by asking them what they need. I had to learn the hard way about assuming. Ask your customer what they want from you and then give it to them. After I get a good idea of what they want, I will start with a beta group; a small group of women that go through the program for a fairly inexpensive price and in the end, I get their feedback. I love having beta groups because they have no problems sharing what they liked and didn't like and what I should do differently, and sometimes this even includes increasing the pricing.

Utilizing surveys and a few beta groups have allowed me to zoom in on my ideal client and give her exactly what she needs every time. After six months of trial, error and more research, I finally started to get everything down to a science, and I immediately began to see results. The language that I used to speak to my ideal client has become more precise, as I now speak directly to her in a language that she understands. Enrollment in my courses began to increase when I made these changes, which meant an increase in revenue for my business.

Another tool that helps you to stand out from the crowd is when you take the time to develop relationships with your ideal clients. Start with small talk and listen to what they share with you. Ask questions and learn all that you can about them. When you develop a relationship with your ideal client that equates to trust. People are more willing to give their money to someone that they know instead of giving it to a total stranger. Now I've had salespeople to argue me down about this concept on social media, but think about what I am saying for just a second. If your best friend and a total stranger were standing side by side and were selling the exact same product, who would you make your purchase from? 9 times out of 10, it would be your best friend. Why, because you know and trust them.

Engagement is another key element that allows you to stand out from everyone else. Do you have a favorite celebrity that you follow on social media? Have you ever commented on one of their post and one day, out of the blue, they commented back? How did that make you feel? Yes, you were on cloud nine, and nobody could tell you anything. Well as you begin to grow, your followers on social media become very important. Take out a few moments to respond to messages that people send to you, even if it is you directing them to visit your website. Respond to comments that people leave on your social media posts, instead of hitting the like button and moving on. People feel special when you take a moment to acknowledge them, and that special feeling can go a long way and also make a difference between you closing a sale or sitting in your home office wondering why no one is buying anything from you.

Staying in business and being a successful owner isn't as easy as social media will lead you to believe. Being an entrepreneur means you have to sit down and actually do the work. You have to learn who your ideal client is, identify their pains and problems, speak their language and begin to develop a genuine relationship with them and then sell directly to them and only them.

Next, I want to take a moment and talk about the importance of referrals. If a customer likes your work, they will refer others to you. Hence, it is very important to have good customer service. Make all of your customers feel special and let them know that what you have to offer is one of a kind; sure, they can receive coaching from anyone with a shingle hanging outside of their door, but it's the experience that makes you unique. Their experience with you should be phenomenal, that when they attempt to work with someone else, they will compare their services, products and most importantly, the way you made them feel. If it doesn't compare they will return to you and they will bring others with them. Also, encourage your customers to refer their friends. A great way to do this is to offer incentives. Give your customers a discount or offer an affiliate program where they receive a percentage of every sale from the customers they refer to you.

Selling is a process that involves guiding the customer through a series of steps that lead them to making a purchase. This is called a sales funnel. A sales funnel is an upside down pyramid that consists of six simple steps:

1. **Awareness** – Your ideal client becomes aware of their problem and they see you have a solution via social media or a Google search. This is where they visit your website for the first time.

2. **Interest** – The client/customer begins to follow you on social media and/or join your mailing list because of a free offer that you have presented to them. They are now gathering data about you and the services you offer

3. **Decision** – The customer reaches a final decision to purchase your product or service from visiting your sales page, attending a webinar you have offered or while speaking with you on the telephone.

4. **Action** – The customer clicks the buy now button and makes the purchase.

5. **Repeat** – They are now a loyal customer and make additional purchases in the future.

6. **Promote** – The customer becomes a brand advocate and now tells others about your products and services.

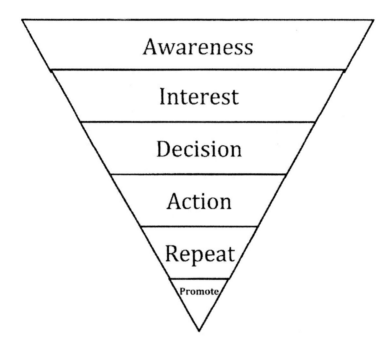

*Sales Funnel*

There should also be at least a 4 to 1 ratio of adding value before asking for the sale via email or social media.

1. **Add Value** – Share an article that pertains to your area of expertise

2. **Add Value** – Talk about a problem that you solved through a story. (everyone loves a good story)

3. **Add Value** – Share one of your favorite quotes
4. **Add Value/Ask for the Sale** – Share a client testimony and end with you directing your ideal client to call, click the link, visit your website and make the purchase.

The art of selling includes consistently adding value to the lives of your ideal customer, educating them, leaving them wanting more and you asking for the sale. As you can see from the sales funnel, this can be done via social media post, but also through emails and webinars. Yes, make sure you are capturing the emails of your ideal clients. Social media sites can shut down today or tomorrow, and your ideal client will be lost, sometimes forever. Another downside to strictly using social media is the follower who is following 500 other businesses that are similar to yours. Connecting with them through email offers you a better chance of having your message seen by them and connecting on a more personal level. First, make sure you are utilizing the services of a marketing automation platform and email marketing service like MailChimp, Constant Contact, or Convert Kit. I have used Constant Contact in the past, and I currently use MailChimp, which offers a free service. These platforms allow you to capture the emails of individuals who visit your website and send out mass emails to your list. It is important to remember when building your website, to have your developer install a drop box to capture the emails of your visitors and offer a tripwire, a free or special offer that entices your website visitors to sign up for your email list. Gone are the days of CC'ing everyone in one email. You are running a business. Everything has to be professional, including the emails that you are sending out to your ideal client and customer.

Webinars can be presented on platforms such as Zoom, Go To Meetings and Webinar Jam. A webinar is similar to a mini course. They are usually an hour long and you present on a certain topic that pertains to the product or service you are selling. Webinars incorporate screen sharing (allowing the participant to see your computer screen) or power point slides. You can offer a webinar for a small price tag of $20–$47 or you can allow participants to attend at no cost. The price factor should be determined based on the financial goals of your business. I normally charge a small fee, in the range of $20–$35.

Now let's talk about your slow seasons. I hate to break it to you, but there will be times when your business will slow down to a snail's pace. This doesn't mean that you should slow down and stop putting yourself in front of your ideal client/customer. Use your slow seasons to continue to give your niche market valuable content. Continue to show up consistently and remind them why they are loyal to you. This is also a good time to collect data; ask them what content they would like to see you create next. Use this time to create new products for your ideal client, but most importantly, engage, engage, and engage so when things do pick back up, and your ideal client/customer is ready to invest in themselves, they will remember you.

As you are preparing to have a successful business remember that it is essential to know who your ideal client is. Everyone doesn't want what your business offers. Your job is to focus on the small part of the population who need what you have and offer a solution or relief to a specific problem that they have, which becomes your niche. You are not trying to make all of the money in the world, but if you become laser-focused on your ideal client and connect with them through social media and emails, you will create the income that you desire.

*"In order to be irreplaceable one must always be different."*

**Coco Chanel**

## *Chapter Five*

If you don't plan to succeed, then you are planning to fail. It's that simple. Many want to be entrepreneurs and have these awesome plans that they never implement. Hence, they are always talking about owning a business, but never move past the planning stage. Plans are awesome. I support having a plan 100 percent, but they are just random thoughts that are floating around in your head until you put some elbow grease behind them. So what do I mean by that?

I highly recommend that once you've identified your niche and your ideal client, and how you can solve their pain, your next step should be to develop a plan of action. An action plan is essential to the success of your business. Unlike a business plan, an action plan takes each big goal that you've set for your business and breaks it down into measurable steps with dead-lines. I also add rewards to my action plan. After accomplishing each step, I have rewards in place that I, or my team, will receive if that particular step is completed. Like a behavior modification plan that we use with children when trying to get them to engage in positive behaviors, small incentives keep the motivation and energy high for yourself and your team. It promotes creativity and a willingness to work harder. Hey, just like kids, adults like to be rewarded when we get something right too.

I look at business plans as just another way to kill a forest. It's a bunch of words on paper that you will eventually forget about. Business plans are great if you are planning to apply for funding for your business, but come on, let's keep it 100, most small business owners are financing their businesses off of a wing and a prayer, and many are using funds from their 9 to 5 to help keep them afloat. Rarely, in the beginning, are we walking into a bank wearing lipstick and heels asking, "can you invest in my dream?" But with the help of an action plan, the possibility of you walking into a lending institution in the future becomes realistic.

An action plan for a business is usually broken down into monthly goals with weekly action steps. Some entrepreneurs use white boards to track their progress, others use project management programs like Trello, while I use a form that I developed. Sorry, but I am a paper and pen type of girl. Each week I have steps that I have to complete that will ensure that I reach my large goal. This tracking system allows me to hold myself, and my team accountable. With one quick glance, I can see if we are heading in the right direction, if something needs to be reworked and if we need to scratch a goal altogether. Utilization of an electronic project management system allows everyone to see the same thing at the same time. As the CEO, you can track the progress of team members and make reassignments if necessary.

Another accountability tool that I use in my business is the old fashion team meeting. I think it is important for your team to be able to feel and see how energetic you are. This is a major part of the hustle for your business, having those around you to exude your excitement and to feed off of your energy. I usually have my team meetings at a nice restaurant, and I pick up the bill. I have a set agenda that will be discussed, and everyone gives an update on what they are working on. This allows us to move from behind a computer screen, freely ask questions, fellowship and strengthen our bond. If you want your team to be loyal, you have to show that you appreciate them.

I have also utilized group text messages and emails, but that can become too much sometimes, especially when people decide that they need to vent and they use this space to do it. I also hate it when my phone is constantly buzzing, and my mind has switched gears. If this is a good way for you to communicate with your team then by all means, use it.

Essentially, remember that planning is just as important as, if not more important than the other suggestions that I have given in this book. Develop a road map that will help you and your team to continue to move in the same direction on your business journey. Work together instead of apart. Hold one another accountable and step in when someone is struggling or if necessary, re-examine why that isn't working and if it needs to be scratched. Create a family atmosphere for your team and most importantly, always let them know that you care about them and that you value their contribution to your business.

*"Many women live like it's a dress rehearsal. Ladies, the curtain is up, and you're on."*

**Mikki Taylor**

## *Chapter Six*

Once I was sitting in a team meeting like the one I mentioned in the previous chapter, with my manager at the time. Although he had worked with some big names in the entertainment industry, and I respected him and his craft, when he decided to tell me to sit down, shut up and just continue to look cute, in front of my team, I had to set him straight. I have always been and will continue to be not only the face of my brand but also the brains behind it. My brand has never come across as just a pretty face with no substance, and I wasn't about to let him take it in that direction. As you bring on team members, you have to be crystal clear about your brand and be able to translate that to others in a precise way. You also have to be clear about your role as a leader.

As women, we are great at organizing our homes and making sure everyone knows their role and that everything is decent and in order, but when it comes to the world of business, many of us have difficulties transitioning into leadership positions. We often doubt ourselves, and our capabilities and will allow a man to step into the spotlight, while we shrink into the background. This is your business, and you have to learn how to lead it. No one will see your vision the way that you do, so it is up to you to step up and make sure your business operations are being handled appropriately, because in the end, if something happens, it doesn't matter who the leader is, the owner is the one that the public see's and will blame.

If bossing up is difficult for you, it is probably due to your lack of business knowledge or some self-worth issues. Start by enrolling in some leadership classes. You can check with your local chamber of commerce or the Small Business Administration. I would also suggest joining a few Facebook groups that focus on entrepreneurship. These are great environments to ask questions and learn from like-minded individuals. Over the years, I have benefitted from participating in mastermind groups and courses that focused on different aspects of running a business. This is also one of the main reasons that I became a business strategist and began to offer the New Entrepreneur Master Class and the Being Boss Boot Camp, so women like you can begin to fearlessly walk in their purposes and run their business like a true boss.

In the beginning, everything will fall on your shoulders, and those who work under you will be depending on your guidance.

Always remember that this is your business and your vision. Every decision will come down to you. Recognize that this is your time to step into the spotlight and begin to utilize all of the skills and talents that you have developed over the years and use them as you lead your team and yourself while building a dynamic business.

*"Option A is not available. So let's kick the sh\*\* out of option B."*

**Sheryl Sandberg**

# *Chapter Seven*

Next, let's talk about marketing and branding. These are two different aspects of business that are dependent upon each other. Marketing is how your ideal client learns about your business and the services/products that you offer. Branding is what people think of you and your business when they hear your name or the name of your company. Many people choose to brand their business, and in the past, that was also my perception as well. But when you know better, you do better. Over the years I've learned to embrace who I am and build my brand around me. Why, because I am my company. When I first started out after quitting my job, everyone naturally wanted me to work with them as a life coach, and I tried it for about three months before I quickly decided that was not the route I wanted to take. As I began to shift my mindset to move further and further away from becoming involved in the inner workings of a person's personal life, I realize that many of my clients were coming to me because they were struggling in their careers and were at a point in their lives where they wanted to quit their 9 to 5's and start a business. They didn't know what to call it, but they valued my knowledge and sought out my services. This was when I realized that they wanted to work with me because of my brand. And this revelation allowed me to shift from life coaching to business coaching fairly easy, which in the beginning, had been a struggle.

Building a brand takes time and consistency, with consistency being the keyword. Your message has to stay the same. This is how people will remember you. My message has always been to empower, inspire and uplift others, but especially women of color. Every article and post that I share on social media points to this message, so when you hear my name you immediately think of those three words which make up my mission statement. Even as I transitioned from one area of coaching to another, my brand has remained the same. I still work with women, and I empower them. Now I empower women by teaching them about entrepreneurship. I inspire women to start their own businesses while feeling good about the decisions they are making. Again, my brand is still the same. My message has not changed.

Branding also consists of having a strong work ethic. You will always be working on your brand. You don't build it and then walk away. Everyday you have to remind people who you are and what is your purpose. This means that you will have to develop a system that includes scheduling social media post, sending out emails and putting yourself in front of your ideal client every single day.

Branding should also carry over into your marketing. Your colors and logo should be the same on all social media platforms and on all of your promotional materials. You should also use the same profile picture on all social media platforms as well, because this makes it easier for people to find you. Many look at your picture first and not your name. Be consistent.

Let me give you an example of branding gone wrong. There is a service provider that I follow on social media. I begin to follow them because their message was about leaving your 9 to 5 job and living a carefree life, doing what you've always wanted to do. They would showcase interviews done with professionals who embodied this concept and were now living in exotic places and running their businesses from their laptops. It was refreshing to watch what they were doing and showing the world that this lifestyle is possible through the stories of others. Then their post began to change drastically. One day they were speaking about religion and quoting Bible scriptures, and the next day, the message was about healthy eating. "What happened to living a carefree life, sitting on a beach, drinking fancy drinks?!" The last time I checked, their posts had shifted once again, and now they are focused on bringing professionals from helping backgrounds together on a resource site. None of these tie into their carefree living brand, instead, their message is scattered and all over the place. It appears confusing, which means they are confused and everyone who is following them is just as confused too. People rarely stay loyal to confusion, unless you are a gossip site and even they are consistent with bringing you drama!

Now let's talk about this beast called social media as a marketing tool. I hear so many women complain about social media and how they aren't comfortable using the platforms because of pettiness and mess. First of all, you are using social media for all of the wrong reasons, if that is your concern. Stop cyberstalking to be messy and posting subliminal messages and start maximizing your post for dollars. Yes, I need you to start using these free platforms to put your business in front of your ideal client and start making your coins.

It's okay to post some aspects of your life on social media because this shows that you are authentic. Just make sure that your "me moments" are an extension of your brand. Mix these moments with sharing content and valuable information that your ideal client/customer can use. This gives your social media page a sense of freshness. Why? Because everyone else in your industry is beating them over the head with buy, buy, buy. Your content will be different and consist of sharing, this is me, here is some valuable information, how are you feeling, and THEN hit them with, "hey, I have this great product that I'm sure you'll love!"

I like to incorporate storytelling. As I mentioned earlier, I have found that buyers are more willing to spend money with you when they feel they can relate to you. The easiest way to build a connection with your ideal client/customer is through storytelling. Invite them into parts of your life by sharing a short story about you. Remember, everything that you do needs to tie into your brand. So stop complaining about social media and start using these platforms as a way to engage with your audience, share content and then ask for the sale.

The last point that I want to make about branding and marketing is to be original. When you go out and copy the messages and branding others are doing, you are reinforcing their brand instead of building your own. Stop worrying about what the entrepreneur sitting next to you is doing. Stay in your own lane and focus on building your own brand, so people remember you!

Finally, everyone isn't going to get you, and that's okay, that just means they are not your ideal client, but everyone should have a clear picture about your brand, and when they say no to your product or service, it is because they understand this is something that they do not need. Be consistent with your message and what you are telling people. When you are all over the place, you appear confused, and people are not going to stick around while you try and figure it all out. Lastly, realize that over time, as your business begins to grow and your revenue increases, your brand will evolve, and that is okay. As you grow as a business owner, your brand is supposed to grow too.

*"People say that money is not the key to happiness, but I always figured if you have enough money, you can have a key made."*

**Joan Rivers**

# Chapter Eight

The reason you should start a business is to serve others by walking in your purpose, but in serving others, your business should be able to cover its overhead and allow you to live the lifestyle that you desire. Many have this negative mindset when it comes to money; they believe and look upon those who profit from a business as being immoral, greedy and selfish. Society has brainwashed us into believing that you should only have enough money to pay your bills and anything over that is excessive or, if we don't have enough, but continue to serve others as we struggle in silence, that God will bless us even more. If this is your mindset when it comes to money you will have a hard time being successful as a business owner. Why? Because you will unconsciously allow yourself to only reach a certain point financially and not go a step further. This is not a good mindset to have. Always giving your time and services away for free is not a good thing. Yes, it is okay to give back when you have the additional resources, and God has placed it on your heart, but don't let people guilt trip you into giving everything away for free. Making money is a reason that we all go into business, and it is nothing to be ashamed of. Your ideal client will find the resources to pay for your solution to their problem, always remember that.

I didn't have to read a book to know that in order for any of my businesses to be successful I needed to have financial goals. Earlier, I talked about having an action plan. Your financial goals should be a part of that plan. When deciding on your business goals each month, as the owner, you should have financial goals that your company needs to meet in order to break even, meet payroll and be able to take care of other financial obligations such as inventory. Essentially, you should have financial goals that you want your business to reach that will allow you to have a reserve of money. A reserve becomes necessary to cover unexpected expenses that will occur because they will. These goals should be higher than your breakeven goals and if reached, put into savings in case you have a month where you don't reach your financial goals.

In the past, I have always operated businesses that required me to be present in order for money to be made, hence if I was falling short of my financial goals I had to physically be present in my business for more hours. This included owning a physical bookstore, a mental health private practice and photography studio. If I wasn't there, then none of the businesses made any money. Even when I transitioned into business coaching, I started out offering one-on-one coaching to clients. When it came to meeting my financial goals, I had to work with a lot of clients each month just to live. This became exhausting. I soon found myself reaching out to other coaches, who informed me that I needed to charge more for my services, which would allow me to make the same amount of money, but see less people. I quickly took their advice, but the problem with this scenario was that my ideal client was not willing to pay the higher price point and that's when I began to look into passive income, and restructuring my active income by offering group sessions and live virtual courses. With group sessions and courses, I am able to work with a large number of people, which, for me, equals an increase in revenue. The price point for individual sessions vs. group and live courses are drastically different, with the later two being less expensive, but these formats allow me to work with more people and free up my time to do other things.

Since implementing passive income, I now have more time to spend with my family, and I generate more revenue vs. when I was working with clients one-on-one. My motto has become, "let my business work for me, instead of me working for it." My ultimate goal each month is to generate enough passive income where I don't have to physically show up every day in order to make money in my business. This has required me to take the resources and skills that I acquired as a business owner and college professor and begin to develop virtual courses and products that now generate income 24 hours a day, 7 days a week because essentially that's what passive income is.

In the past year, I've learned how to recycle products that I created and continue to generate revenue from them. One example is *Sideline Ho*, the novel I released back in 2007. I still receive income from this book and all of the books that I've written since then. I don't have to rewrite them, but I do have to remind people where they can find them and that they are still for sale. My books are listed either on Amazon or my own website, and I make sales 24/7 without me having to be present. I have also taken teleconferences and courses that I've taught live and turned the recordings into products that women can purchase as digital downloads and utilize in the comfort of their own homes without me having to physically show up and teach the classes again.

I also generate income by having sponsors for my podcast on iTunes, *Beauty, Brains, and Business.* Businesses pay a fee to have me promote them on episodes of my show. Once the recording is made my producer places it on each show and that's it. All the business has to do is renew the sponsorship each month, and my show generates passive income. We don't have to keep recording the commercial over and over again, but it continues to generate income for a segment of my business.

Another form of passive income that I also utilize is affiliate marketing. I actually have an entire course on this topic on my website. With affiliate marketing, I share resources in the courses that I teach and share a link where the participants can sign up to utilize these resources. If they make a purchase using the link that I shared with them, I make a small percentage off of the sale. It's not a large amount, but it adds up when considering income for my business. This is a source of passive income because I only have to share the link with them one time. I have also used this type of passive income for my podcast and YouTube videos.

Again, the idea is to generate revenue while I am doing other things, including sleeping. My goal is to no longer be tied down to my business and working long hours just to make money. That's partially why I never returned to the workforce. Passive income allows you to generate income while working on other parts of your business, spending time with your family or sitting on a beach drinking a Mojito.

Now when I create a product, I not only think about how I will utilize it at that moment, but how I can later recycle it and turn it into a source of passive income. CiCi Gunn, the founder of The Six Figure Chick, often states in her webinars that when developing a product, set an overall financial goal of how much revenue a new product has to generate. This goal may include offering a course live, then turning it into a digital download that is sold by itself and then eventually selling it in a bundle package. You should map out the financial revenue for each product that you will sell for approximately one year. Yes, narrow down your financial goals to the exact dollar amount each product needs to generate. This will allow you to see where your income will come from as you work towards your yearly financial goals.

I have this saying, "never throw anything away when it comes to content." I firmly believe that everything can be repackaged and utilized in a different way to generate income. I challenge you to go through products you've created and think about how you can recycle them and begin to generate revenue while you are sleeping. I also challenge you to map out the different ways you can sell the same product for one year. Write this number down and make it a financial goal for that product.

Here is an example of repackaging and maximizing financial revenue for one product. Take products from your physical store and start selling them online through a virtual store. Now orders can be placed 24/7 and all you have to do is package and ship them out twice a week and then offering them in a buy 1, get one for 50% off (bundle). Another idea is creating digital downloads. You can upload manuscripts for workbooks that you have previously released as paperbacks, on a digital marketplace or your website and charge people a fee to download them. You do not have to create a new product, simply use, recycle and maximize what you have already created. Again, once you've made the product and placed it online, no additional work is required on your part except reminding people where they can go to get their copy. The idea is to work smarter, not harder.

I hope this chapter has helped you to begin thinking outside of the box when it comes to generating revenue for your business and streamlining your process. Start allowing your products to work for you, instead of you having to show up every day and be present to generate income as a business owner. Take a moment to look at the products and services that you currently have and begin to develop creative outlets that will allow you to recycle them and continue to make a profit. Always remember, generating wealth should not stifle your flexibility, but instead increase it.

*"You can't please everyone, and you can't make everyone like you."*

**Katie Couric**

## *Chapter Nine*

Lisa Nichols once said, "you have to be willing to completely die from any form of who you have been to become who you are supposed to be." Everyone and everything has a season in your life, and only a few will last a lifetime. This is a hard concept for many to accept. We often want to take the old us; habits, friends, and mindsets into the future with us and because of who you will and have become, she will become a misfit and begin to block the blessings of the new you.

If you aren't a successful entrepreneur it is because you are standing in your own way, it's just that simple. The woman that you are isn't the woman you are supposed to be. You need to change. You need to grow. You need to let some things go, but you are having a hard time doing so.

Becoming a successful entrepreneur means that you have to shed the dead skin that you've been growing in. This means that you will have to change some habits. This means you may have to let some people in your life go. This means you may have to become more uncomfortable before you can begin to become comfortable. It means you will have to learn how to be loyal to yourself first and then to everyone else.

Here I was, an educated woman with three degrees yet, I had experienced a nervous breakdown from remaining in an unhealthy job situation one day too long, I was flat broke and I was alone. I had a closet full of every shade of black clothing that you could think of, some that still had the tags on them. The black represented the depressive state that I had been in for a while. It's funny now when I think back, because I never realized that every piece of clothing I was purchasing was black. I was mourning the death of something, but it wasn't until that moment, while standing in the middle of my closet, that I realized a part of me had been trying to die for a long time and I kept refusing to give her permission, letting her know that it was okay.

At that moment, I realized that it was time to let go and so I packed up 80% of my closet and dropped the items off at Style Encore, a resale shop for professional women. I swear I must have taken them over $1,000 worth of clothes, but ask me why I was excited when they handed me a check for $107.00. Now the old me probably would have complained and told them to give me my clothes back, but I wasn't that woman anymore. I didn't need all of those items to work out of my home office every day. All of my meetings were now taking place via telephone and Zoom. When I thought about it, I mainly wore sweats, shorts, t-shirts, and flip-flops. So I didn't complain. I said thank you and used the money to buy grocery for my sons and put gas in my car. But the feeling that I remember as I walked out of that store was humble and grateful. I realized that I had purchased all of those clothes to make me feel good, but in the end, they helped me to feed my kids and get them to and from school for a week. That meant I had another week to try and get my business where I needed it to be. That meant I was that much closer to making something, anything happen. And so I brushed off my ego, got back up and kept trying.

Other things that I let go of as I transitioned into a full-time entrepreneur included people. I had a few girlfriends whom I considered my ride or dies, but when they saw me going downhill emotionally, they slowly begin to fade away. I didn't realize it for a while, then one day I noticed they had stopped accepting my calls, were not returning my text messages and if they happened to answer when I called, they quickly rushed off of the telephone with a bougie Black girl attitude. When I finally realized what had happened, I broke down and cried like a baby. These where supposed to be my girls, "you bring the gun, I got the bullets," yet here I was at rock bottom, and they were nowhere to be found. But once I dried my eyes, I accepted the fact that they were not supposed to go where I was going and that their season in my life had ended. As I blocked their phone numbers, I thought about the scripture that my mother would often quote to me before she passed away, the scripture that was read at her funeral, Ecclesiastes 3:1-8:

There is a time for everything, and a season for every activity under the heavens:

A time to be born and a time to die,

A time to plant and a time to uproot,

A time to kill and a time to heal,

A time to tear down and a time to build,

A time to weep and a time to laugh,

A time to mourn, and a time to dance,

A time to scatter stones and a time to gather them,

A time to embrace and a time to refrain from embracing,

A time to search and a time to give up,

A time to keep and a time to throw away,

A time to tear and a time to mend,

A time to be silent and a time to speak,

A time to love and a time to hate,

A time for war, and a time for peace.

Yes, I blocked their numbers, because I knew from past relationships that people have a tendency to come back when they think you are doing better when it looks like you're on top. I knew that the new me no longer needed those kinds of friends nor that kind of validation in my life. So I moved on without them.

I also realized that shedding means letting go of certain mindsets. Yes, there's that word again, mindset. Let's talk about the negative mindset that many of us currently have. Don't look around; I am talking to you. Since becoming aware of what a negative money mindset looks like, I can now spot it anywhere and on anyone, especially on social media. Just the other day I put a post on LinkedIn discussing how Kim Kardashian West made $10 million dollars in one day, selling a perfume that no one had ever smelled. I expected the negative comments because let's face it, Y'all just be hating on Kim K, but that's another story for a different book. But what caught me by surprise was the people who took the religious route and talked about preferring to have morals, values and good character instead of $10 million in the bank. They got the side eye. First of all, there are a lot of people in the world with $10 million dollars or more in their bank accounts, and they still drive a Honda Prius, live in an ordinary neighborhood and attend church every Sunday. Second of all, if you are not BFF's with Kim Kardashian, I am going to need you to sit down and stop judging her. This woman is a wife and mother, and yes, she sold $10 million dollars in perfume, not coochie, not porn tapes, not a mega church where the pastor ran off with the money, not music that refers to women as bitches and hoes. As Plies said, "You mad. You big mad." And you also have a problem with money. You also have some self-esteem issues which are affecting your relationship with money as well.

There is nothing wrong with having a bank account that looks like a phone number, versus a zip code and if you believe otherwise, I am going to need you to sit down and ask yourself why. Why do you believe that it is morally correct to be on the struggle bus 24/7? Why do you believe that if another woman is out there making her coins and money that folds, that something is wrong with her? The reason is that deep down inside you really wish that you were her. Now you don't have to admit it to me, but take a moment and be honest with yourself. When you see her success, you grow green with envy. You suddenly feel that she is unworthy and then you begin to find everything wrong with her for being the success that you are not. Maybe this mindset has to do with a traumatic event that you experienced in your life and never got over. It could be that you have issues with other females because of unresolved issues that you have with your mother while growing up. Maybe you were bullied, told that you would never be good enough, smart enough and so you begin to believe it. Whatever your reason(s) is, please take out some time and work with a therapist to help you move past those issues so you can get out of your own way.

Another reason that contributes to poor money mindsets is that many of us, including myself, grew up with poor examples when it comes to getting money, keeping money and taking that money and making more money. I grew up in a household with parents that argued about money, so I believed that money made people angry. But I also saw my parents hustle and work their full-time jobs while running a family catering business on the weekends. I learned that when money gets tight, you fall back on the skills and talents that you've always had and a side hustle just in case mad day comes at your 9 to 5, and they decided that they no longer need your services.

While married to my second husband, money was used to control me. He would take the money from our family businesses and hide it from me, and I would have to ask for money to buy groceries (if he didn't take me to the grocery store and purchase everything himself.) I also had to ask for an allowance that often would not cover basic necessities for myself and our two sons. When we were going through our divorce proceedings, I was informed by my lawyer that my now ex-husband had 50k in a separate bank account and that I was not entitled to half because it was an inheritance he had received and he had never co-mingled the funds with money we shared together. After putting myself and our two sons out of the family home that we rented because he had led me to believe that we couldn't afford to buy our own home, my ex gave me a cashier's check for $2,500 to get an apartment, but to my surprise, when we arrived in court a copy of the check was submitted as him paying child support along with falsified tax returns showing that he only made $12,000 a year, which drastically lowered his future child support payments. Believe me when I tell you that my mindset with money went from bad to worst. It would take me years to overcome the hurt and pain that I had experienced when it came to money, but if I wanted to live a better life, it was something that had to be done.

Becoming the entrepreneur that I am today and having several successful businesses required that I learn how to make money, keep money and then grow that same money! I had to stop overspending and learn how to tell my kids no sometimes. After having a nervous breakdown, I knew that going back into the workforce was not an option, so I tackled this problem head-on. I listened to the audio book Rich Dad, Poor Dad. I began watching YouTube videos on mindsets. I attended webinars on how to generate passive income, and I studied business moguls like Kim Kardashian, Tony Robbins, Lisa Nichols, and Gloria Mayfield Banks who are multimillionaires. I threw away the mindset that everything was a scam, and I started to listen, take notes and do my own research.

I also begin to realize that the $48,000 job I had just left was an insult. That the salary I had allowed them to pay me, was a gross misrepresentation of what I was really worth, but before I could begin to make six and seven figures, I had to let go of my five-figure mindset. I had to release the hurt and pain that I associated with money. I had to break the bondage that kept me with a slave mentality of depending on a 9 to 5 to survive. I had to develop a boss chick way of thinking to get to the next level of success.

I also had to get honest about the lifestyle that I wanted to live and figure out how to get it. Again, I go back to Mrs. West. She wants to live a fabulous lifestyle that includes jet-setting around the world, being a mom, having nannies, dying her hair blonde if she wants too, wearing designer names from her head to her toes and living in an ultra-fabulous mansion with her husband and their family. So she gets up everyday and takes her inspirations and turns them into million dollar creations that we, the consumer buy. I had to get to that level. I had to make it happen too!

In all honesty, I could live a Kim Kardashian West or Kris Jenner lifestyle and y'all could say whatever you wanted about me and I wouldn't care. Why? Because I would be living the life that I created for myself, just like they did. If you've been following me for a while, then you know my ultimate goal is to develop my business where I can run it from a laptop while sitting on a beach enjoying a beautiful sunset and sipping on a fancy drink. So if I want that lifestyle, I have to create it. I have to figure out how to generate enough revenue that will allow me to live it and create a legacy that will allow my children and grandchildren to live it too. So no, I'm not mad at Kim for making $10 million dollars in one day. Instead, I'm looking for her marketing blueprint with a flashlight in the daytime, because she has figured out how to create the life that she wants to live and she is living it!

In order to become the woman that God has intended for you to be, you must first let go of the woman that you have become. You have to change your mindset, especially if it is negative around certain issues and figure out why it is that way. You must also invest in yourself and your growth. Don't expect anyone to give you anything for free. And besides, you'll appreciate it even more. Let the current you die, so you can give birth to the boss chick you are meant to be.

*"We need to accept that we won't always make the right decisions, that we'll screw up royally sometimes—understanding that failure is not the opposite of success, it's part of success."*

**Arianna Huffington**

# *Chapter Ten*

I 'll be the first to admit that I am far from perfect, although a lot of people try to place me on a pedal stool or put me inside of a box of perfection, I am always honest with myself. Yes, I sometimes have grammar errors in emails and on my website, and that happens when you are trying to get work done at 4am in the morning. Do I apologize for not being perfect? No. I am human just like everyone else, and I have never allowed my imperfections to stop me, and neither should you. It is because of these imperfections that we are unique and that what we each bring to the table is special. Yes, I've made my fair share of mistakes, especially when it comes to business, and if I want to continue growing, I will continue to make mistakes. Because mistakes allow you to grow and they mean that you are trying new things to improve who you are and where you are and figuring it all out along the way.

One mistake that I made early on was assuming that everyone was cheering for me. Just because someone is on your payroll doesn't mean that they want you to succeed. At one point I was changing assistants like I changed my underwear. I've dealt with people stealing money at events, managers who thought I was their property even though I was the one signing their paychecks, workers having an attitude when I questioned what they were doing and why they were doing it, and sometimes it all became too much. I'll admit that sometimes I just threw my hands in the air and let people do whatever because I was tired of dealing with them and was secretly hoping they would just quit. But eventually, I had to boss up if I didn't want my business to fail and find the strength to fire them. After I had the assistant who breached my conflict of interest clause, I realized that people really don't care about you, your tribe, your team or seeing you win. I learned the hard way that you have to remind yourself that your employees are disposable, and if they aren't doing what you need them to do and what you've asked them to do, then it's okay to show them to the door. Don't hold on to excess baggage and employees because, in the end, they will only bring you down.

Another serious mistake that I made in the past was, not knowing my worth. When I look at my resume and see almost six years of free training and speaking engagements that I provided, I could kick myself in the butt. I left so much money on the table being nice, feeling sorry for people and quote, unquote, building a name for myself, but not realizing that I was already known. After two years, I really should have started charging to do public speaking engagements. At that point in my career, I had several books under my belt, and I had built a reputation for myself. The problem was that I didn't know my worth. Hence, I now preach to everyone that I work with to never leave money on the table and to always value yourself and know your worth when it comes to business because no one else is going to step in and let you know that you are valuable and that you really should be getting paid. If they do, they are a rare diamond that you should treasure forever!

My next mistake was putting passion over profits. And when I say passion, I am referring to men and romantic relationships. Yes, I was that woman who would fall in love, and the world would stop moving. I would become inconsistent and begin to shift all of my focus on him as if he was "the one." And the truth be told, none of them were ever, "the one." I messed up by giving them husband privileges when they were just casual dates. My advice to you, don't stop what you're doing when it comes to your business because of any type of relationship. Instead, find a healthy balance. It is okay to be supportive, but always put your oxygen mask on first and make sure your business is breathing before you decide to help someone else breathe. And if a person doesn't try to understand or tries to discourage you, you need to exit them from your life too.

My last big mistake was not being private enough. I've done a good job of keeping my kids out of the media. They didn't ask for this life, and so I've worked hard to maintain a sense of normalcy for them. But sometimes I would go on rants on social media about my relationships and other stuff that really shouldn't have been aired out that way. I've learned that 1) people are going to talk about you no matter what, and you can't argue with all of them, and you surely can't care, 2) if you put it on social media it's no longer private and people will dig up stuff from years ago and try to throw it in your face, and 3) there is nothing social about social media. It is a trap that will suck you in if you let it. I now utilize social media to market my business, and anything else will have to be developed outside of the Internet. If I need to rant, I do that with a friend. If I am in my feelings, I go see my therapist.

Learn how to use social media the right way instead of being petty, throwing shade, gossiping and hating on others or as a source of therapy. Use your health insurance and go see a therapist or check out Talk Space, an on online site where you can work with a virtual therapist for a small cost. But whatever you do, just remember that social media is not meant for you to air your personal business.

If you keep putting off starting a business or growing your business because you want everything to be perfect, you will always be in the idea stage, versus the ownership stage. Rome wasn't built in a day and neither will your business. Allow yourself to make mistakes, because that is a sign that you are trying. Learn from your mistakes and use that information to elevate you and your business to the next level.

*"No matter what you're going through, there's a light at the end of the tunnel, and it may seem hard to get to it, but you can do it, just keep working towards it and you'll find the positive side of things."*

**Demi Lovato**

# *Conclusion*

S tarting a business will be challenging. In the beginning, you will have more bad days than good days. These will be the days that test your strength, determination, and motivation. And it will all come down to one thing, "how bad do you want it?"

I hear so many women talk about these great ideas, but never implement them. I see women start businesses but then watch in horror as they self-destruct on social media or fall to the demise of a relationship that fails just as fast or faster than her business. I understand the woman who has the negative mindset when it comes to money, but then she loses me when she refuses to get help. And the woman who finds comfort in tearing down other females who are out there making things happen, simply because she is afraid to deal with her own insecurities. I've had to deal with her on so many levels, hoping that one day she will see that we are in this thing together. I wrote this book so you won't be any of these women and if you are that woman, you can do better because now you know better.

It is my hope that you will use the information that I've presented on these pages, to help you to become the boss chick that God intended for you to be. I pray that you will share this book with other women who desire to leave the 9 to 5 rat race, but don't know where to start and are wondering why they should even try.

I hope I have dispelled the myths that entrepreneurship is easy and that the women who run these businesses are flawless and without any imperfections. I want you to see and understand that if you want to be successful in business, you have to start somewhere, wherever that may be. You have to work through your issues, fall on your face, and realize that it is only a failure if you never get back up. Yes, you will cry, you will cuss, you will delete people from your life and you will survive, but you will also grow, and you will become the entrepreneur that God intended for you to be. So put on your lipstick and heels, and let's start hustling.

# *Meet The Author*

D
r. Carey Yazeed is a Business Strategist who specializes in working with women who are tired of the 9 to 5 rat race and desire to be their own boss. A graduate of Louisiana State University with a Ph.D. in Higher Education Leadership and Research and Tulane University with a Master Degree in Social Work, her business experience includes operating a mental health private practice for 20 years, in addition to co-owning a barbershop, bookstore and photography studio. She is the current owner of Shero Productions, a virtual boutique that includes her business coaching, publications and trainings for women. Yazeed currently resides 60 miles outside of New Orleans, in a rural part of South Louisiana with her two sons and their 3 pets. For

more information about the author or to have her speak at your next women empowerment event, please visit her website at www.drcareyyazeed.com